Practical advice, in bite sized pi

I0076744

QUICK
SALES TIPS

SUSAN A. ENNS
ROBERT J. WEESE

MANAGING PARTNERS
B2B SALES CONNECTIONS

ISBN: 978-0-9876928-4-9

DEDICATION

To all the successful sales professionals we have been lucky enough to work with over the years. Each of you has taught us something that has made us better.

"I truly believe that everything that we do and everyone that we meet is put in our path for a purpose. There are no accidents; we're all teachers - if we're willing to pay attention to the lessons we learn, trust our positive instincts and not be afraid to take risks or wait for some miracle to come knocking at our door." – Marla Gibbs

Quick Sales Tips
By Susan A. Enns
Robert J. Weese

INTRODUCTION

Desmond Tutu once said, "Do your little bit of good where you are; it's those little bits of good put together that overwhelm the world."

It's true isn't it? Change seldom happens in the blink of an eye. More often than not, it's all those little changes that happen along the way that, when added together, end up having the most impact. For your health, it's "an apple a day keeps the doctor away." For your financial stability, it's "a dollar a day for the rainy day." And of course in sales, you hear "a new prospect a day keeps the sales manager away." The same is true for your own personal development. You have to invest a little in yourself on a regular basis to truly see improvement over the long term.

"Quick Sales Tips" is a collection of little ideas to help you realize your sales potential. Simply put, this is practical advice, in bit sized pieces. Whether you are an entrepreneur marketing your own products and services, or a direct sales representative servicing your assigned sales territory, this book will improve your skills so you will sell more.

Did you know studies show 25% of sales reps produce 90 to 95% of all sales? Clearly, most sales people are not selling up to their potential, and not making the incomes they could, nor producing the revenues they should.

Why is this case? It's not that the job can't be done because 25 percent are doing it, and doing it well. It's because the other 75 percent either are not in the right sales position or they truly don't know how to sell. If all sales people knew and did what the top 25 percent do, then all sales people would be selling more!

B2B Sales Connections wants to change that. We are an online sales training website with free sales resources, a specialized sales job board and free resume listing services for business to business sales. You could say we specialize in helping b2b sales professionals achieve their sales potential, either by connecting them to the right career choices, or the right skill set. Our website is b2bsalesconnections.com.

When we started the company a number of years ago, we realized that one of the best ways to improve people's sales skills was to distribute a monthly sales newsletter filled with sales tips, techniques, and best practices. The glowing feedback we received from the readers of *"AIM HIGHER"* was overwhelming and our subscriber quickly grew, as it continues to do so today.

One of the most popular sections of the newsletter has always been our monthly quick sales tip, dating all the way back to our first edition. It was when one subscriber wrote us and said, "... if sales folks would follow your "sales tip of the month" every day...their life would change" we decided to put all our best tips in one place and the idea for this book was born.

"Quick Sales Tips" is based on over 50 years of successful B2B sales and sales management expertise. It is a collection of our own personal sales techniques, as well as other successful sales professionals we have been lucky enough to work with over the years. They are in no particular order, just a random collection of over 100 tips to help you achieve your sales potential. We hope you find them as influential on the success of your career as our newsletter subscribers have found them to be.

When you retire and look back on your career, you will realize it was the small improvements to your skills and techniques you made over the years that made the most difference on your overall success. But of course you already know that. That's the reason you are reading this book. So let's get started!

QUICK SALES TIPS

"Improve by 1 percent a day,
and in just seventy days,
you're twice as good."
 - Alan Weiss

Sales Tip# 1

- Think you don't have time to spend on on-going personal development? Did you know that if you read for just 10 minutes a day, that is over 60 hours per year! If you a looking for a great read, we have some great book suggestions on our website at http://www.b2bsalesconnections.com/books.php

Sales Tip# 2

- No one returning your voice mails? That's probably because you are speaking too fast! When you are leaving your phone number on a voice mail, write it down at the same time. That will ensure you speak slowly

enough so that your voice mail recipient will
be able to write it down too!

Sales Tip# 3

- You really only get paid for the time you
  spend selling. Always ask yourself, "What is
  the best use of my time right now?"

Sales Tip#4

- Carry with you at least 2 blank copies of
  every type of paperwork your prospect must
  sign to process your order. That way you
  won't have to make a return trip if you
  happen to make a mistake. More
  importantly, you will always be prepared to
  close the sale whenever your prospect says
  yes!

Sales Tip# 5

- Should you answer your cell phone or PDA
  in a sales call? Most people consider it rude
  if you do. To paraphrase an old saying, one
  face to face prospect is worth two on the
  smart phone! Yes, technology has opened
  up a whole new world of possibilities for us.
  However, just because you can doesn't
  mean you should!

Sales Tip# 6

- What time should you arrive for an appointment? Obviously you should not be late, but you should not be too early either. Being more than 10 minutes early makes your contact uncomfortable knowing that you are waiting so long before your appointment.

Sales Tip# 7

- Tired of voice mail tag? Leave a detailed message on your first call, including the request you want to make. That way, if you are not available when your contact calls back, at least they can leave you the answer to your question on your voice mail.

Sales Tip# 8

- Give out 2 business cards to every contact. That way your contacts can refer you to associates and still keep a card for themself.

Sales Tip# 9

- When you make a sales call, be sure to stop in and cold call the companies on either side and across the street from your original call. That's five calls every time you park the car!

Sales Tip# 10

- Don't arrive on Monday morning and ask yourself "what am I going to do this week?" Work this week to book your appointments for next week!

Sales Tip# 11

- Experience has shown that the other sales reps in the office will not buy from you! So don't spend more time talking to them than you do potential customers!

Sales Tip# 12

- Are you doing the same things over and over again? Automating your routine with proposal templates, automatic price calculators, and email templates can free up more selling hours in your day! We also have some great automated tools for the sales professional, the sales manager, and channel sales manager on our website at http://www.b2bsalesconnections.com/auto mated_tools.php

Sales Tip# 13

- Find time to do just one more call a day. That is 260 calls a year, or an extra month to make money every year!

Sales Tip# 14

- Time spent in the car is not productive, so minimize it. Book your appointments so you work your territory geographically. For example, if you have a sales presentation scheduled for next week, prospect to book other appointments in the same postal code or zip code on the same day. This also has the added benefit of saving on gas too!

Sales Tip# 15

- Do you regularly receive updates to important computer files like price lists? Add the date to the file name when you save it. That way, you will ensure that you are always using the most up to date version!

Sales Tip# 16

- Need to create a sense of urgency with prospects? Make sure you put an expiry date and other time deadlines in all of your proposals!

Sales Tip# 17

- Just like meetings with customers, schedule at least an hour of prospecting time in your calendar each day. Open your next week's calendar and book it now! Then stick to it, to matter what!

Sales Tip# 18

- Your customer's perception is your reality. Don't waste your time writing proposals just for the sake of writing proposals. If they don't see a problem, there is no problem!

Sales Tip# 19

- When is it acceptable to use abbreviations or acronyms with a customer? If it is a generally understood abbreviation, then it is acceptable. For example, GST is a common term. However, if the abbreviation is a company or industry specific term that you only learned when you started selling your product, then don't. If you didn't know its meaning before joining your industry, chances are your prospect won't either. When in doubt, don't use the abbreviation!

Sales Tip# 20

- What is the purpose of your sales call? What do you specifically want to accomplish? How will you know if it was a successful sales call? If you can't answer these questions because you do not have a pre-planned agenda, you are only wasting yours and the prospect's time!

Sales Tip# 21

- Think back to the last sale you made. In what industry does that customer operate? Perhaps other companies in that industry share the same problems. More importantly, perhaps they would share the same benefits from your solution. Why not pick up the phone and find out? Vertical marketing works!

Sales Tip# 22

- What are you distinct competitive advantages? You will drastically increase your chances of winning the sale when together you and your prospect identify problems that you can fix better than the competition.

Sales Tip# 23

- Having trouble staying motivated? Divide your sales results or earned commissions by the number of prospecting calls you complete. Knowing how much each prospecting call is worth to you will help keep you going.

Sales Tip# 24

- If you need to keep a mileage log, and most of us do, simply enter your starting and ending odometer reading in your day timer or PDA each day. At the end of each week, month, or year, simply subtract the opening and closing mileage readings.

Sales Tip# 25

- How do you tell your prospect your price? If you add adjectives like "our usual price", " the suggested list price" or "our regular price", you are actually inviting the prospect to negotiate and ask for a lower price. Instead, try "the price is" and simply state the fact.

Sales Tip# 26

- When you are introduced to someone, do you shorten their name? Do you say Tom when meeting Thomas? Stop! Many people don't like their names shortened without their permission. It is much safer to ask, "Do you prefer Tom or Thomas?" than to just assume.

Sales Tip# 27

- Do what you say you are going to do, when you say you are going to do it. Breaking a commitment to a customer is worse than never having made the commitment in the first place.

Sales Tip# 28

- Can you describe what you do in 30 seconds or less? Most sales reps can't. The best elevator speech answers the question, "what does a good referral look like?"

Sales Tip# 29

- Professional athletes always go through a pre-game warm up to ensure they are mentally prepared to perform at their best. So should sales people. Before you enter your prospect's office, take a moment to get your head in the game!

Sales Tip# 30

- Do you ever wear a name tag at a networking meeting or trade show? The proper place to pin your name tag is high on your right side. That way, it is in the natural line of sight of the person you are meeting when you shake hands.

Sales Tip# 31

- Don't always leave the same voice mail messages for prospects. Script a series of voice mails, each with a different benefit statement. With persistence, sooner or later one benefit message will induce the prospect to return your call.

Sales Tip# 32

- After a networking event, send a quick hand written note saying "Great To Meet You" to every business card you collected. Include in the note your definition of what an ideal referral is for you and invite the person to share your contact information. You will be amazed at the positive feedback you receive. This truly will set you apart.

Sales Tip# 33

- Where ever possible, delegate non sales related activities like service calls and customer care inquires to the people in your company who specialize in them. For example, don't place a service call for the customer, show them how to do it themselves. Remember, as a sales person, you are the quarterback of the team, you are not the whole team. Your time is best spent selling!

Sales Tip# 34

- Pre-call research, either on the internet or from other sources, is great but don't overdo it. The extra information you find given the time it takes away from selling may not be worth it. Sooner or later you are going to just have to pick up the phone and call the prospect!

Sales Tip# 35

- Have you ever received a great compliment from a customer that you wished you could share with others? Just ask the customer, "Can I quote you?" When he says yes, add it to a list of all the other great compliments you have received, and hand it out to prospects. Such a testimonial list is a very powerful sales tool!

Sales Tip# 36

- Is your prospect just too far away to meet with face to face? Schedule a phone appointment at a predetermined date and time. If you plan properly, these appointments can be extremely productive in moving the sale forward, not to mention the time you saved not having to travel!

Sales Tip# 37

- Never open a cold call with "Hi, how are you today". Nothing warns a gatekeeper that you are just another sales person making cold call faster than that statement. If you are using this as your opening, change your headline and watch your results improve!

Sales Tip# 38

- Stop taking phone calls from prospects when you can't devote your entire attention to the caller. It is very frustrating when you ask the prospect to call you back later because you can't take notes right now as you are in the middle of a meeting or travelling in your car. The customer would have preferred to leave you a voice mail with their request on their first call rather than having to ask you again on their second call.

Sales Tip# 39

- Add related products to your sales proposals. The reason McDonald's™ employees always ask you if you want some fries with that is because many people say yes. Remember, suggestion selling works!

Sales Tip# 40

- Take the time to plan your prospecting sequence and manage the timing of it in your CRM system. The first step could be an introductory letter, step two a phone call a week later, and step three could be a follow up email that same day. Once defined, it becomes just a matter of implementing your system.

Sales Tip# 41

- Your voice mail is not only a message taker, it can also be a sales tool. Most times prospects and customer hear your message before they have a chance to talk to you. Why not seize the opportunity to leave a brief marketing message? "Ask me about our new widget that will save you..." can generate interest and give you something to be discussed when you return your customer's call.

Sales Tip# 42

- You don't always have to answer a customer question in person to be effective. Sometimes an after-hours voice mail message with the requested answer not only satisfies your customer, it can save you valuable selling time as well.

Sales Tip# 43

- Cell phones can often cut out. When listening to your voice mail, sometimes all your recipient can hear is "613-???-?295". They have no way of calling you back if they wanted to! Always say your phone number twice, once close to the start of the message and again at the end.

Sales Tip# 44

- Is your sales quota important enough for you to hold it dear to your heart and make it the driving force in your life? Probably not. Take the time to set your own goals and create a plan of action to achieve them. What is your desired lifestyle? How much income must you earn to fund that lifestyle? What sales activities must you complete every day to earn that income? Answer these questions and you are well on your way to getting where you want to go! To help you calculate the your goals and create a plan of action to achieve them, download our *GOAL SETTING & ACTION PLANNING TOOL* from the B2B Sales Connections Free Download Centre at http://www.b2bsalesconnections.com/down load_centre.php

Sales Tip# 45

- Not sure how you sound on the telephone? Leave a co-worker a voice mail message just as you would for a client, and then ask them for feedback. You can also call your own voice mail to hear how you sound. Did you speak slowly enough? Could they write down your phone number? Does your message say "tell me more" or does it say "whatever, good-bye"?

Sales Tip# 46

- Do you track your sales activities? Some sales people think that tracking their activity on sales reports is nothing more than a policing action so the boss can check up on them. The most successful sales representatives look at sales reports differently. They see them as their GPS navigation system on the road to achieving their income and lifestyle goals. Do you know what you need to do today to get to where you want to go? Shouldn't you?

Sales Tip# 47

- The person you are calling may not have your phone number handy when they listen to your voice mail. Therefore, no matter how well you know the person; always leave your phone number.

Sales Tip# 48

- When you are leaving a voice mail, don't rhyme off your name so fast that the person must listen to the message more than once to get it. Chances are they will delete it before they will listen to it again. Slow down and always speak clearly and more prospects will return your calls.

Sales Tip# 49

- Do you know how many proposals you must present in order to make a sale? If you don't, how do you know you are making enough presentations to reach your sales goals? If you don't know how many you need, download our *GOAL SETTING & ACTION PLANNING TOOL* from the B2B Sales Connections Free Download Centre at http://www.b2bsalesconnections.com/down load_centre.php

Sales Tip# 50

- It is wrong to believe that every company can and will buy from you. In the same way that sports fans see mostly beer commercials and Saturday morning cartoon viewers see mostly toy ads, you must target your prospecting efforts. Review your past sales to clearly define your target types of companies. Once you know your targets, spend your time where you are most likely to find them!

Sales Tip# 51

- It is dangerous to believe that every company in your target market can buy from you at any time. Know how often your prospects buy your products, or how often they renegotiate the contracts for their use. Knowing where your targets are in their buying cycle will ensure that you are not only you in the right place, but also there at the right time!

Sales Tip# 52

- Do you have a large database of companies and contacts stored on your laptop or PDA? A database that is sorted alphabetically, even if it is the most advanced electronic type possible, is just a glorified phone book. Sort your database by the date of your next sales call and check it daily. A database itself doesn't make you money. It's what you do with it that does.

Sales Tip# 53

- Do you track all of your prospecting contacts in contact management program? Make sure you enter every call, regardless of whether they are a prospect or not. Not only it is important for you to know where to go when, but it is also important to know where not to go.

Sales Tip# 54

- What do your customers have in common? How many employees do they have? What industries do they operate in? How often do they use your product? When you start to track your past successes, you can identify commonalities that help you define who is most likely to buy from you in the future.

Sales Tip# 55

- When you track commonalities and characteristics about your customers, is your list exhaustive? In other words, can every company be classified using your list? If it isn't, you are not gathering all the information you need to.

Sales Tip# 56

- The ultimate goal of any business is to make a profit. Absolutely everything a company buys affects its bottom line. Even a pencil that lasts longer, or is less expensive than the previous one purchased helps a company to make more profit. Help your customers get to where they want to go by showing them how your product helps them make more profit!

Sales Tip# 57

- If you sell a simple or transactional product where the customer can make the buying decision very quickly, don't write the price on a brochure when the prospect asks for a quotation. Write the price on an order form instead. Not only will this give the prospect the information he has requested, but it will save a lot of time because the sale will close much more quickly.

Sales Tip# 58

- Regardless of how expensive or complicated your product is, a written proposal should not be longer than 6 pages. Too much information can actually slow or halt the sale, not move it forward. Your prospect only needs just enough of the right information to make a logical buying decision. Did you need or want detailed blueprints of framing, plumbing and electrical wiring before you bought your house? Neither does your prospect!

Sales Tip# 59

- Successful sales representatives know that templates are a huge time saver when creating proposals. All that should be needed to customize a proposal for a particular prospect is to change the customer information and the financial considerations. Many studies show that sales people only spend about 25 percent of their time selling. If you have a $1 million quota, your time is worth $2,000 per hour. Use it wisely!

Sales Tip# 60

- Has your trade show budget been slashed? Is your display just another way for your competitors to check you out? No new prospects visiting your booth, only those you invited to the show? Host an open house instead! It is less expensive, takes less time to set up, and it can be much more effective at closing sales than some trade shows.

Sales Tip# 61

- Do you carry a portfolio binder with you when you are on sales calls? Why not turn it into a pitch book with copies of reference letters, customer lists, and other testimonials. That way you are always prepared to build your credibility whenever the need or opportunity arises.

Sales Tip# 62

- Do you ever wonder if your email was received? With today's spam filters, it's a valid concern! To keep your sales process moving forward, phone the recipient the day after your send the email (or fax) and ask if they have received it. Regardless of the outcome, your follow up call will build your credibility and you will move your sales process forward. Any way you look at it, that's a good thing!

Sales Tip# 63

- Do the unexpected. People are used to poor follow up and lack of customer service. When you exceed their expectations, you set the bar higher than your competitors.

Sales Tip# 64

- Studies show that 2 out of 3 sales are made to customers who have said no not once, but 5 times! Yet 75% of sales people give up after just the 1st or 2nd rejection. It is easy to see why 25% of all sales people produce 90 to 95% of all sales.   Don't give up too early. Persistence pays!

Sales Tip# 65

- Take notes. First of all, no one can remember everything a prospect says. Secondly, you never know when you are going to need to refer to a past conversation with a prospect to help move the sale forward.

Sales Tip# 66

- Carefully plan out what you are going to say before your next sales call. After all, even an Academy Award winning actor takes the time to rehearse his script before he can make it look natural when the cameras start to roll.

Sales Tip# 67

- Heading to a networking meeting? Before you jump into the car, make sure you bring a good supply of your business cards and some breath mints.

Sales Tip# 68

- Never call a prospect or customer and say, "Hi Fred, I am just calling to see how things are going." or "I'm just calling to touch base." People are busy and don't have time for this casual contact. When you make contact, make it important and beneficial to the other person. For example, "Hi Fred, you popped up in my follow up file today. When we last spoke..." is very effective as a greeting.

Sales Tip# 69

- In music and sports, the rule is practice, practice, practice. In real estate it's location, location, location. In sales, it's follow up, follow up, follow up.

Sales Tip# 70

- Use an automated signature for your emails that includes your return email address, your phone number and any other contact information that is important. Don't make your prospect hunt for your contact information when they find something in your email that makes them think, "tell me more!"

Sales Tip# 71

- If a prospect doesn't know you, they need to know what other people think about you. Why? Because a prospect won't buy from you unless they think they can trust you.

Therefore you need to use testimonials. Use them often and use them everywhere.
Simply put, you can never provide too many testimonials!

Sales Tip# 72

- If you are having trouble getting to a C-level executive because their assistant will not connect you, call early in the morning before 8:00 am of after 5 pm. These people work longer hours than their assistants, and often personally answer their phone outside of normal business hours.

Sales Tip# 73

- To stay in better contact with your social networks, create lists or tags that correspond to each month of the year. File each of your contacts on one of the lists and then call them in the month you assigned to them.

Sales Tip# 74

- People want to deal with local businesses. Use that to your advantage when possible.

Sales Tip# 75

- People buy on emotion and then justify with logic. This means your message must connect on an emotional level first. You need success stories about how you helped a customer reach their goal or solve a problem before you talk specifications.

Sales Tip# 76

- Taking a call on your cell phone or texting during meetings is inappropriate. It doesn't work to hide your phone under the boardroom table either. Everyone in the meeting sees you looking down and it is very obvious that you have lost focus.

Sales Tip# 77

- Whether it's for networking meetings or prospecting calls, have a couple of elevator pitches ready for the different products or services you represent so you can focus your approach on your target market with each one.

Sales Tip# 78

- Be excited. It's contagious.

Sales Tip# 79

- When a prospect or customer tells you about a problem, think "Which means" and then ask follow up questions so you know exactly what is causing the pain. "Tell me more" is another great way to get customers talking!

Sales Tip# 80

- Always be a little better dressed than the people you are working with. Wearing a golf shirt to an appointment where white shirts and ties are the norm will not make a good first impression. Similarly, if you are dressed in formal business attire and the customer is a t-shirt person, then loose the tie and jacket.

Sales Tip# 81

- Find out if the prospect is really in the buying cycle or just kicking the tires and playing the "What if" game. Improve your pre-qualification process to avoid wasting time preparing proposals for prospects who really won't buy right now anyway!

Sales Tip# 82

- Don't write notes on scraps pieces of paper or post it notes. You need to keep all your notes in note books that are dated and filed for future reference. You will be glad you did some day.

Sales Tip# 83

- A prospect is not interested in your product pitch; they just want to solve their problem. Tell them how you can do that in simple to understand descriptive terms. Using complicated technical terms and specifications is not only unnecessary, it actually does more to hurt the sale, than help it.

Sales Tip# 84

- Studies show that over 70% of the time when the prospect says "your price is too high", they really mean they don't trust you and just want an easy excuse to get rid of you. Someone will always be cheaper - so be better!

Sales Tip# 85

- Web surfing while dining, be it with business associates or friends, is not acceptable. Besides, isn't the whole point of social networking to connect with people? It's more effective to connect with the person sitting across from you rather than tweeting about who you are with.

Sales Tip# 86

- Join Toastmasters™ to improve your presentation and leadership skills.

Sales Tip# 87

- If you meet someone at a networking event that you would like to begin a business relationship with, then take the time to impress them. Find out some current event affecting their industry and then send them some pertinent information on the subject along with a handwritten note. You certainly will receive a warm reception when you make a follow up call.

Sales Tip# 88

- Never assume you know the solution. Sales people can jump to conclusions too fast.

You must wait for the customer to state their problem and its implications before you can move to your solution. Don't skip steps in the sales process because the prospect needs to go through them for his buying process as well. After all, better the fact find, happier the customer, better the pay check!

Sales Tip# 89

- Don't go to networking events expecting to walk away with a bunch of business cards for potential customers. Attend networking events to become known as an expert in your field. Your goal should be to become known and seen as a go to person. The sales leads will come in due time.

Sales Tip# 90

- Pattern your voice to that of your prospect. If they speak slowly and take their time to think about their next thought, you need to move slowly as well. Likewise, if someone is moving and speaking at a very fast rate of speed, you should mirror the quick pace.

Sales Tip# 91

- If you are emailing back and forth with a customer or business associate and the subject matter of the email changes from the original topic, change the subject line to reflect it's a new discussion. You can even note that you have changed the subject line right in the subject line itself. This essentially starts a new email string which makes it will make it easier for everyone to follow and refer back to it days, weeks or even months later.

Sales Tip# 92

- Don't automatically offer a discount when a customer asks for one. Justify your value first. Before you drop your price, ask the customer what they would like to remove from the package. Psychology proves that people would rather pay more than lose something they see as valuable to them.

Sales Tip# 93

- If a discount is unavoidable, choose an odd number like 3.5% as opposed to a round number like 10%. It will show that you were not over priced in the first place, and will make the discount look like it has a very specific reason. Remember though, a discount that makes a sale lose money is not worth it. If it not profitable, don't offer it.

Sales Tip# 94

- Don't be afraid to say, "I don't know, but I will find out the answer and get back to you." Better to admit this than to make a promise that you won't be able to keep.

Sales Tip# 95

- Everything doesn't have to be perfect before you get started. Pick up the phone and make the calls. You will get better with every call you make and it will become easier with every person you speak to. After all, you don't wait for all the traffic lights to be green before you back the car out of the driveway every morning do you?

Sales Tip# 96

- When presenting documents to a prospect for signing, let them take the time to read things over without your interruption. Too many sales people give the prospect a few seconds and then start selling again. Don't talk yourself out of a sale. As the old saying goes, ask for the order and then shut up!

Sales Tip# 97

- Your prospects, customers and colleagues don't care or need to know about your personal problems. Shake them off and be a professional with a positive attitude.

Sales Tip# 98

- Business etiquette dictates that when you are using a speaker phone or hosting a conference call, you should announce who else is in the room.

Sales Tip# 99

- "Having trouble keeping all of your receipts you need for tax purposes organized? Create a file folder for each of these categories: Automobile (gas, parking, washes, insurance etc.), Charitable Donations, Home Improvements, Internet Service Charges, Meals, Medical, Office Supplies, Other, Postage, Telephone/Cellular and Utilities. Put your receipts in the appropriate file at the end of each day. When it comes time to submit your taxes at the end of the year, all the sorting is done!

Sales Tip# 100

- Never be afraid to walk away. If you are not the best solution today, don't make the sale today. In the end, you will build more credibility and are far more likely to gain the prospect as a valued client in the future.

Sales Tip# 101

- Always carry with you two pens because chances are, when you are in the middle of signing that big contract, you pen will run out of ink. As the Boy Scouts always say, "Be prepared!"

Sales Tip# 102

- Watch your prospect's body language. When you see a questioning look or a look of surprise, stop and find out why.

Sales Tip# 103

- When making a presentation, you are better to have three to four main points that relate directly to your prospect's problem rather than having 10 standard product benefits. Not only will your prospect identify more with your solution, but people don't usually remember more than that anyway.

Sales Tip# 104

- Fire bad customers. Every business relationship must be a win-win in order for it to survive long term. If the relationship is not profitable for you or your company, it is best to part ways.

Sales Tip# 105

- When you meet someone, make eye contact, smile, and give them a firm hand shake. Gentlemen, don't dislocated the person's shoulder by shaking too hard. Ladies, the palm of your hand should be perpendicular to the ground, and your hand should not bend at the knuckles.

Sales Tip# 106

- If you use online social networks like LinkedIn, Facebook or Twitter, create templates in Word for messages that you send over and over again. That way you can just copy and paste them into the network's message box. Not only does this save a lot of time, but it also ensures you don't have any spelling errors because most social networks don't have spell check.

Sales Tip# 107

- Create a "Recurring To Do List", with separate categories labeled Daily, Weekly, Monthly and Ongoing. Place all of your regular to-dos in the appropriate category. For example, if you need to complete 10 new sales contacts each day to reach your sales quota, list it in the Daily category. If you want to connect with one new social network contact each week, put it on the Weekly category. As you check things off your lists, not only will you gain an incredible sense of accomplishment, but you will be well on your way to achieving your goals and objectives.

Sales Tip# 108

- Do you have a prospect that once was very engaged with your sales process, but now won't return your calls? Send them an "is it time to close your file" email. You will be amazed at how many will let you know that something unexpected and urgent has changed their priorities and then give you a date for you to follow up and renew your contact with them. For an email template that you can use to restart a stalled prospect, download our *EMAIL TEMPLATE TO RESTART STALLED PROSPECTS* from the B2B Sales Connections Free Download Centre at http://www.b2bsalesconnections.com/download_centre.php

Sales Tip# 109

- Send out thank you cards. Not only does it let your valued clients know you appreciate their business, but it is also a great opportunity to ask for referrals.

Sales Tip# 110

- Don't be afraid to leave a voice mail. The chances may be low that you will receive a return phone call, but those chances are higher than if you just hang up the phone and never leave a message in the first place. You are there anyway. Why not leave a voice mail? Remember the rule of 3 in 18. It states that a prospect has to hear of your company name at least 3 times in 18 months before they will even remember your name. A voice mail, even though they don't return you call, counts as one of the three touches.

Sales Tip# 111

- Find a mentor or a coach. Musicians, professional athletes and business leaders all rely on mentors throughout their careers to help them develop professionally. You should too.

ABOUT THE AUTHORS

"Those who say it cannot be done are
usually interrupted by those already doing it."
- James Baldwin

SUSAN A. ENNS

Susan is a Managing Partner
of B2B Sales Connections,
the sales coaching website
with free sales resources,
online sales training, a
specialized sales job board,
and free resume listing
services for business to
business sales professionals.
She brings over 26 years of
direct sales, management
and executive level business to business
experience. Her accomplishments include
consecutively being the top sales rep in Canada,
managing the top sales branch, and achieving
outstanding sales growth in a national channel
sales organization.

Before co-founding B2B Sales Connections, Susan
gained marketing, sales and general management
experience in the business technology and office
equipment industries. She also has experience in

the group insurance industry, as well as owning and operating her own businesses.

Some of Susan's career highlights include:

- Directed two regional sales operations simultaneously to outstanding sales growth
- Increased a regional sales operation to 39% average annual sales growth over a 5 year period
- Achieved 374% of profit targets as Branch Manager
- Managed the top branch in Canada, with consistent year over year record sales results
- Operation selected as a finalist in the Better Business Bureau Torch Awards for Marketplace Ethics
- Sales Representative of the Year for two consecutive years before being promoted to sales management

Susan has received her Bachelor of Commerce (Honours) degree from the Faculty of Management at the University of Manitoba, where she was named to the Dean's Honour List in three separate years. She is also a Certified Internal ISO Auditor.

She has written training courses for sales and sales management, created numerous automated sales tools, and as the B2B Sales Coach, she writes and edits the company's newsletters.

For many years, Susan has volunteered on numerous executive committees of professional associations, sport leagues and clubs in which she's been a member. She has volunteered on the organizing committee for Canadian Breast Cancer Foundation CIBC Run for the Cure for several years, currently as the Volunteer Co-Run Director, herself being a breast cancer survivor after being diagnosed in 2013. She was also an annual participant in the Canadian Cancer Society Relay for Life for several years.

She volunteered on the Leadership Executive of the Sales Professionals of Ottawa (SPO) for 5 years, and is one of the association's Past Presidents. She has also been a guest lecturer at the School of Business at Algonquin College as well as a guest speaker for SPO.

Λ competitive athlete from an early age, she is a Kinsmen Award Winner for Good Citizenship, Sportsmanship, and Hard Work. Now an avid golfer, she has been voted Most Sportsmanlike Player and All Star Skip in separate curling leagues.

By creating and teaching various sales training courses, coupled with the innovative creation and implementation of useful sales tools, Susan has excelled and been recognized in all areas of her personal and professional endeavors.

Other Titles from Susan A. Enns

Discover these titles from Susan A. Enns, Managing Partner of B2B Sales Connections at www.b2bsalesconnections.com

Not just what to do, but how to do it!

ACTION PLAN FOR SALES SUCCESS

SUSAN A. ENNS
MANAGING PARTNER
B2B SALES CONNECTIONS

ACHIEVE YOUR SALES POTENTIAL!

Action Plan For Sales Success - Not just what to do, but how to do it!

Learn sales techniques used by today's top producing sales professionals. Action Plan For Sales Success will improve your selling skills so that you can achieve your true sales potential.

Not just what to do, but how to do it!

ACTION PLAN FOR SALES MANAGEMENT SUCCESS

SUSAN A. ENNS
MANAGING PARTNER
B2B SALES CONNECTIONS

ACHIEVE YOUR SALES POTENTIAL!

Action Plan For Sales Management Success - Not just what to do, but how to do it!

By learning the techniques used by today's top producing managers, you and your team can achieve your true sales potential!

If misery loves company, then motivation breeds happiness!

DAILY MOTIVATIONAL QUOTES

SUSAN A. ENNS
MANAGING PARTNER
B2B SALES CONNECTIONS

Daily Motivation Quotes - If misery loves company, than motivation breeds success!

This is a collection of favourite motivational quotes. Some are sales related, some are business related, but most are simply life related. They are in no particular order, just a random thought for each day of the year to help keep you on a positive note.

What people are saying about Susan:

- "Our company hired Susan in mid 2011 as our sales coach. I have been working with her since then. She has helped me make more appointments, close more deals and make more money. The 3 most important concepts in sales. I would recommend any sales force hire her to help boost business sales and build trust and integrity with your clients."

- "Susan really knows the selling world. She's honest, articulate, bright, giving, highly competent, personable and a top professional. Welcome her. It's the right thing to do."

- "Susan ...understands the sales process intimately and is able to create a management process around it that drives sales people to accomplish their goals."

- "Susan knows her stuff. She brings many years of great sales experience and success to anyone who wished to improve their skills in sales. She is very personable, and is not afraid to tell it like it is. I would recommend anyone (and I have) to Susan, her website, her books if you want to become a better sales person."

Connect with Susan Online

Connect with Susan online at

- Website: www.b2bsalesconnections.com
- A Sales Compass: A Blog by B2B Sales Connections: http://www.b2bscblog.com
- LinkedIn: www.linkedin.com/in/SusanEnns
- Facebook: www.facebook.com/B2BSalesConnections
- Twitter: www.twitter.com/SusanEnns
- YouTube: www.youtube.com/SusanEnns
- Skype: User Name - susanenns.14

ROBERT J. WEESE

Robert is a founding partner of B2B Sales Connections. He brings over 30 years of direct sales, management and executive level business to business experience. His accomplishments include being named sales manager of the year at a North America business technology company, 100% Sales club of a Fortune 500, and achieving exponential sales growth in a national channel sales organization..

Before co-founding B2B Sales Connections, Robert gained marketing, sales and general management experience in the business technology and office equipment industries. He is an experience broadcaster, an award winning speaker, author, fencing coach and Toastmaster

Some of Robert's career highlights include:

- 39% annual growth over 5 years managing a National Sales division
- Increased product penetration to existing customers to over 20%

- Consistent price attainment within sales group over 100%
- 100% Sales Club member with Fortune 500 company
- Created and delivered dealer sales and product training programs throughout North America
- Developed and implemented successful sales reporting and revenue forecasting systems for sales and executive management use

Robert has received degrees from Trent University & Loyalist College and attends professional development programs regularly to keep his skills up to date. He work has been published several times by various sources.

For more than 20 years, Robert has done volunteer work with disabled and able-bodied athletes. An avid competitive fencer himself, he is the founder and head coach of the Ajax Fencing Club. He is also a member of the Ajax Pickering Board of Trade and Advisor for the Spark Centre for Innovation. He is a respected keynote speaker on business challenges and has received numerous awards and accolades for his volunteer work in the community.

Robert has widespread experience building regional, national, and industry specific sales channels. Both personally and professionally, Robert has demonstrated a proven track record of success.

What people are saying about Robert:

- "We increased our company sales by over 35% this year and have Bob's training program to thank for the focus and success"

- His coaching style and outgoing personality helped make the workshop a positive experience for myself and my coworkers. Thanks Robert for a great workshop and some useful resources that will help increase our sales success."

- "We had been searching for sales agents using on line sales agents job boards and other sources for over two years. In less than 2 weeks Bob was able to connect us with 6 qualified candidates and we signed two immediately and are in discussions with two more."

- "Bob gives his time to answer questions and lend his expertise to me to assist me in building my business. I highly recommend him and his business to anyone!"

Other Titles from Robert J. Weese

Discover these titles from Robert J. Weese, Managing Partner of B2B Sales Connections at www.b2bsalesconnections.com

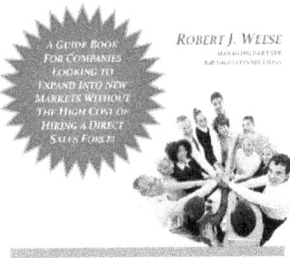

How to Find, Recruit & Manage Independent Sales Agents - Part of the Action Plan For Sales Success Series!

Would you like to sell to new markets and territories using a proven business model without the high cost of adding a direct sales force?

The answer is to find experienced, local sales agents or manufacturers' reps.

This comprehensive guidebook can help you find, train and manage independent sales agents using a proven, turnkey system that will become the foundation of your sales agent program.

Connect with Robert Online

Connect with Robert online at

- Website: www.b2bsalesconnections.com
- A Sales Compass: A Blog by B2B Sales Connections: www.b2bscblog.com
- LinkedIn: http://www.linkedin.com/in/bobweese
- Facebook: www.facebook.com/B2BSalesConnections
- Twitter: www.twitter.com/RobertJWeese
- Skype: User Name - robertjweese

www.ingramcontent.com/pod-product-compliance
Lightning Source LLC
Chambersburg PA
CBHW050530210326
41520CB00012B/2518